YOUR PASSPORT TO

MEXICO

>> by Isela Xitlali Gómez R.
and Anaïs Deal-Márquez >>

CONTENT CONSULTANT

Fernando Riosmena, PhD
Associate Professor of Geography
University of Colorado Boulder

CAPSTONE PRESS
a capstone imprint

Published by Capstone Press, an imprint of Capstone
1710 Roe Crest Drive, North Mankato, Minnesota 56003
capstonepub.com

Library of Congress Cataloging-in-Publication Data
Names: Gómez R., Isela Xitlali, author. | Deal-Márquez, Anaïs, author.
Title: Your passport to Mexico / by Isela Xitlali Gómez R. and Anaïs Deal-Márquez.
Description: North Mankato, Minnesota : Capstone Press, an imprint of Capstone, [2022] | Series: World passport | Includes bibliographical references and index. | Audience: Ages 8-11 | Audience: Grades 4-6 | Summary: "What is it like to live in or visit Mexico? What makes Mexico's culture unique? Explore the geography, traditions, and daily lives of Mexican people"— Provided by publisher.
Identifiers: LCCN 2021028688 (print) | LCCN 2021028689 (ebook) | ISBN 9781663959287 (hardcover) | ISBN 9781666322002 (paperback) | ISBN 9781666322019 (pdf) | ISBN 9781666322033 (Kindle edition)
Subjects: LCSH: Mexico—Juvenile literature.
Classification: LCC F1208.5 .G64 2022 (print) | LCC F1208.5 (ebook) | DDC 972—dc23
LC record available at https://lccn.loc.gov/2021028688
LC ebook record available at https://lccn.loc.gov/2021028689

Editorial Credits
Editor: Marie Pearson; Designer: Colleen McLaren; Production Specialists: Christine Ha and Laura Manthe

Image Credits
Getty Images: Pedro Pardo/AFP, 23; Newscom: Javier Rojas/ZumaPress, 27; Red Line Editorial, 5; Shutterstock: Aleksandar Todorovic, 28, Belikova Oksana, 24, DC_Aperture, 15, FERNANDO MACIAS ROMO, 25, Filip Bjorkman, Cover, Flipser, (passport) design element, Ivan Soto Cobos, Cover, Kobby Dagan, 21, Kuryanovich Tatsiana, 13, Lou Sisneros Photography, 17, Magi Bagi, Cover, Marcos Castillo, 19, MicroOne, (visa stamps) design element, NataliaST, 6, pingebat, (stamps) design element, WitR, 14, Yasemin Olgunoz Berber, 9, Yevhenii Dubinko, (stamps) design element

Printed and bound in China. 5174

CONTENTS

Words in **bold** are in the glossary.

CHAPTER ONE

WELCOME TO MEXICO!

The stands at the market are full of color. There is papel picado. This is paper with patterns cut into it. Vendors are selling fruits and orange Mexican marigold flowers. Families are preparing for Día de los Muertos, or Day of the Dead. They create spaces called altares in their homes. They include pictures of their loved ones who have passed away. They will serve plates of food and drinks on these altares. They will celebrate their loved ones' lives. This is a time of remembrance.

PEOPLE OF MEXICO

Mexico is a country in North America. Its rich traditions go back thousands of years. About 130 million people live there. Mexico has a mix of many cultures. Each culture tells an important part of Mexico's story.

MAP OF MEXICO

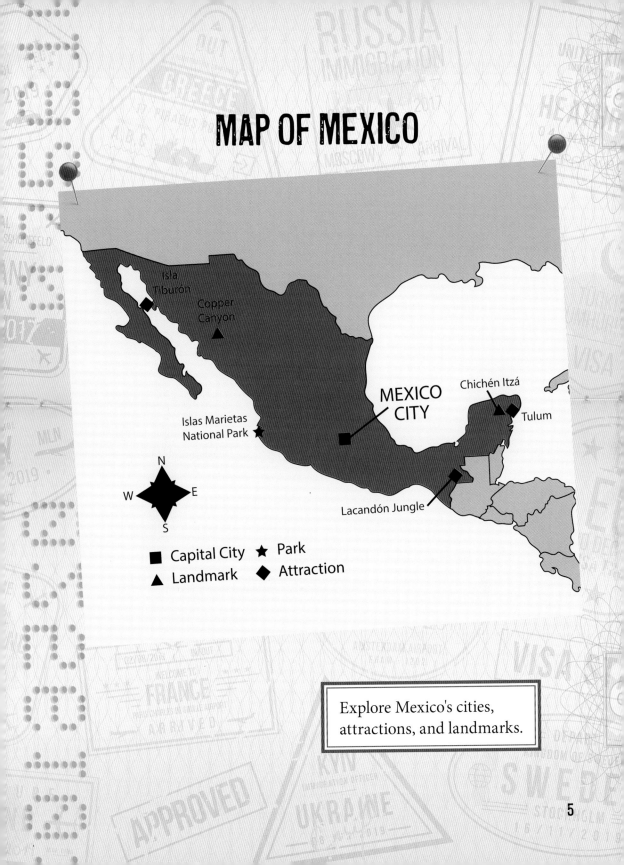

Isla Tiburón

Copper Canyon

MEXICO CITY

Chichén Itzá

Tulum

Islas Marietas National Park

Lacandón Jungle

N
W · E
S

■ Capital City ★ Park
▲ Landmark ◆ Attraction

Explore Mexico's cities, attractions, and landmarks.

Copper Canyon's beauty draws visitors from other countries.

Mexico is home to 78 **indigenous** groups. These people's **ancestors** have lived in Mexico since before the Spanish arrived in the 1500s. For example, Copper Canyon is located in the northern state of Chihuahua. The region has been home to the Rarámuri people since long before Europeans arrived. There are also Afro-Mexicans throughout the country. Their ancestors were enslaved and brought to Mexico. Each region of Mexico has its own geography, food, and traditions.

FACT FILE

OFFICIAL NAME: ....UNITED MEXICAN STATES
POPULATION: 130,207,371
LAND AREA: ....750,561 SQ. MI. (1,943,945 SQ KM)
CAPITAL: ....MEXICO CITY
MONEY: ....MEXICAN PESO
GOVERNMENT: ....FEDERAL PRESIDENTIAL REPUBLIC
LANGUAGE: ....SPANISH; 63 INDIGENOUS LANGUAGES

GEOGRAPHY: Mexico borders Guatemala and Belize in the south and the United States of America in the north. The Pacific Ocean runs along the West Coast. The Gulf of Mexico runs along the East Coast. The Caribbean Sea is to the southeast. The country has mountains, deserts, and tropical regions.

NATURAL RESOURCES: Mexico has petroleum, gold, silver, copper, corn, sugarcane, coffee, wheat, beans, tomatoes, bananas, chiles, and oranges.

The southern state of Yucatán has many cenotes, or natural sinkholes with water. The cenotes were created by the collapse of underground caves. The Maya used the cenotes as a source of water as well as for ceremonies.

CHAPTER TWO

HISTORY OF MEXICO

People have lived in Mexico for more than 10,000 years. The Olmec civilization existed from 1200 to 400 **BCE** on the East Coast. It is one of the earliest known civilizations in Mexico. Later peoples, including the Maya and Zapotecs, may have descended from the Olmec peoples. By 200 **CE**, the Maya had built cities in southern Mexico. In the 1300s CE, the Mexica (Aztec) people built an empire. Its capital was in present-day Mexico City.

FACT

The Maya built the ancient city of Chichén Itzá. It is located in what is now Yucatán. Many people enjoy seeing its large pyramid called the Pyramid of Kukulcán.

The Spanish invaded in 1519. They found thriving cities. The cities had **irrigation**. There were beautiful temples.

The National Museum of Anthropology in Mexico City has many artifacts from Mexico's ancient civilizations.

The Spanish **conquistadores** enslaved Africans and brought them in the early 1500s. Many enslaved Africans **revolted**. They formed their own freed colonies. The history and traditions of all of these groups of people influenced Mexican culture.

TIMELINE OF MEXICAN HISTORY

1200–400 BCE: The Olmec civilization exists in what is now Mexico.

1325–1519 CE: The Mexica Empire builds a civilization at Tenochtitlán.

1519: Hernán Cortés lands at present-day Veracruz. Spanish colonization begins.

1520s: The Spanish start bringing enslaved Africans to Mexico.

1810–1821: Mexico wins freedom from Spain in the Mexican War of Independence.

1824: The United Mexican States are formed.

1829: Vicente Guerrero becomes the second president of Mexico and the first Black president. He ends slavery in Mexico.

1846–1848: Mexico loses land to the United States in the Mexican-American War.

1910–1920: The Mexican Revolution leads to the formation of a federal republic.

2018: Andrés Manuel López Obrador is elected the 58th president of Mexico.

BECOMING A COUNTRY

In the early 1800s, people in Mexico began resisting Spanish rule. They revolted in the Mexican War of Independence. They won their independence in 1821. Three years later, Mexico became a republic. The United Mexican States formed.

The United States of America **annexed** Texas in 1845. Texas had recently belonged to Mexico. This started the Mexican-American War (1846–1848). The United States won. It took even more land away from northern Mexico.

By the early 1900s, many people worked under a few wealthy landowners. Conditions were harsh. In addition, Porfirio Díaz had been president for many years. He had a lot of power. The Mexican Revolution (1910–1920) overthrew Díaz. It led to the formation of a federal republic. But a single party ruled for almost 70 years. Election results were changed in favor of that party. The country has had more accurate election results since the 1990s. In 2018, Andrés Manuel López Obrador was elected president.

FACT

Before the Mexican-American War, modern-day California, Nevada, and Utah were all part of Mexico. So were parts of Arizona, Colorado, New Mexico, Oklahoma, and Wyoming.

CHAPTER THREE

EXPLORE MEXICO

Mexico has many places to visit. Different regions have dry, tropical, or cold climates. Mexico is part of the Ring of Fire. This region has many volcanoes. Most of the volcanoes are dormant. This means they have not erupted in a long time.

SACRED PLACES

There are many places in Mexico that are spiritually important for people today. The city of Teotihuacán is one example. It was built from the first century to the 600s CE. Scientists aren't sure who built it. The ruins are near today's Mexico City. Teotihuacán was more than 8 square miles (20 square kilometers) in size. Many thousands of people once lived there. Today, people can visit this site. They can climb the pyramids.

Popocatépetl is one of Mexico's active volcanoes.

The remains of the Templo Mayor are in the middle of Mexico City.

Mexico City stands on the Mexica capital city of Tenochtitlán. The Templo Mayor is in the heart of Tenochtitlán. This temple was built between 1427 and 1440. Many important religious events took place there. Funerals for state leaders were held there too. Spanish conquistadores destroyed the temple. Today, there is a museum on the site. Visitors can learn more about the history of the city and temples.

Tulum is on the Yucatán Peninsula.

The Maya city of Tulum sits on the southeastern coast of Mexico. The remains of some buildings still stand. They were built between 1200 and 1550. The city was a trading center. People also came for religious ceremonies. Visitors can see the Caribbean Sea from Tulum.

FACT

Mexico City sits on a dried-up lake bed. The soil of the lake bed is softer than the surrounding land. When an earthquake hits, the soil in the lake bed shifts a lot, making it more likely that buildings will collapse.

LAND AND WILDLIFE

Mexico has many places of natural beauty. The Islas Marietas National Park is in the Pacific Ocean. It is off the coast from the city Puerto Vallarta. The park protects the Marieta Islands. Volcanic activity formed these islands thousands of years ago. The islands are popular among tourists. The clear blue waters are home to diverse animals. There are many species of seabirds, dolphins, and rays. The islands are protected from fishing and hunting.

The Usumacinta River cuts through the Lacandón Jungle. The jungle is in southern Mexico. It crosses into Guatemala. The Lacandón is full of beautiful waterfalls. There are also Maya ruins. Jaguars live in the jungle. But more than 90 percent of the jungle has been cut down. Often it has been cut for farming.

COLORFUL LAKES

Lagunas de Montebello National Park is in southern Mexico. There are more than 50 lakes here. Some are deep blue. Others are blue-green. Woodpeckers, toucans, falcons, and quetzals all live near the lakes.

Birds, including blue-footed boobies, live on the Marieta Islands.

Isla Tiburón, or Tiburón Island, is Mexico's largest island. It lies off the coast of Sonora in the Gulf of California. It is the ancestral land of the Seri people. Today, it is uninhabited. The Mexican government protects it as a nature preserve. It is home to coyotes and mule deer. Hunting is managed between the tribal and federal governments.

TWO VOLCANOES

Popocatépetl and Iztaccíhuatl are two volcanoes near Mexico City. There's a legend that long ago, they were lovers. When they died, the gods covered them in snow. They became mountains.

CHAPTER FOUR

DAILY LIFE

There are many types of food in Mexico. Mexican food is often spicy. The kitchen is a place where the family gathers to share recipes and stories.

Meals often include tortillas. They are made from maíz, meaning "corn." Mexican corn has many varieties. It comes in yellow, blue, purple, and other colors. Corn can be used in chilaquiles. This dish is made of strips of fried corn tortillas. The tortillas are simmered with salsa. It can be topped with corn, chicken, eggs, and other foods. Some chips are made with corn. Some drinks also include corn. Soske is a traditional corn-based beverage of the Mascogo people. The Mascogos descend from escaped enslaved Black people and the Seminole American Indians.

Many families in Mexico enjoy preparing and eating meals together.

NOPALES

Nopales is the Spanish word for prickly pear cacti. This cactus grows almost everywhere in Mexico. Some people cook it. Others enjoy eating it raw in salads.

Nopales Ingredients:

- 3 medium nopales, edges trimmed and spines scraped off
- ¼ cup salt
- ½ red onion, thinly sliced
- Juice of 3 limes
- 3 medium tomatoes, cubed
- 2 avocados, cubed
- ¼ cup cotija cheese
- 2 tablespoons chopped cilantro
- ½ teaspoon dried Mexican oregano
- Olive oil

Nopales Directions:

1. Rinse and dry the nopales.
2. Slice the nopales into thin strips. Place the nopales in a colander with salt. Let them sit for 30 to 45 minutes.
3. Rinse the nopales with cold water to remove the slime.
4. Sauté the onions in light oil with half of the lime juice for 3 minutes.
5. Place all the ingredients in a serving dish. Toss the ingredients with the remaining lime juice and a pinch of salt. Add a drizzle of olive oil.

Today, members of a mariachi band often wear matching clothes. The clothes are similar to those of cowboys from the Mexican state of Jalisco.

MUSIC

Mexico's regions have many kinds of music. Mariachi music is one popular kind. It commonly includes guitars, trumpets, and violins. Mariachi music dates back about 200 years.

Son jarocho originated in the state of Veracruz. It developed as a blend of African, Spanish, and indigenous music. It centers around the jarana. This instrument has eight strings. It looks similar to a ukulele.

CHAPTER FIVE

HOLIDAYS AND CELEBRATIONS

Mexicans observe many holidays and celebrations. On September 16, Mexico celebrates its independence from Spain. This day is a symbol of freedom and hope. People enjoy historic reenactments. They watch fireworks at night.

RELIGIOUS HOLIDAYS

More than 80 percent of Mexicans are Catholic. Many towns in Mexico have a **patron saint**. A town celebrates its patron saint once a year. This celebration usually includes a parade to the church. People attend **Mass** there. They eat food. They enjoy traditional dances.

People in Cuajinicuilapa celebrate the patron saint Nicolas of Tolentino.

People dance in parades to celebrate
Día de la Virgen de Guadalupe.

On December 12, Catholic Mexicans celebrate Día
de la Virgen de Guadalupe. This holiday honors Mary,
the mother of Jesus. There are special meals. People
attend Mass. Many towns have parades that include
indigenous dances and music.

People decorate a rosca de reyes with dried fruit and sweet paste.

Three Kings Day is on January 6. It is a Christian holiday. It celebrates the time when the three wise men came to visit baby Jesus. People make rosca de reyes, a circular sweet bread. A small plastic doll is baked into the bread. A family sits with friends to cut the rosca. They eat it with a cup of hot chocolate. Whoever gets the piece with the doll has to host a party in February.

CHAPTER SIX

SPORTS AND RECREATION

Soccer is the most popular sport in Mexico. National clubs have loyal fans across the country. The World Cup is a time for family and friends to gather. Indigenous sports and games are also popular in Mexico. Pelota Purépecha is similar to floor hockey. It is more than 3,000 years old. People still play it today.

ADVENTURE

Many people in Mexico enjoy the outdoors. When it's warm, people spend time by water. They visit the ocean, rivers, or hot springs. Families bring food and drinks to share.

Javier "Chicharito" Hernández Balcázar is one famous soccer player to come from Mexico.

Some people enjoy boating on one of the lakes in Mexico City's Chapultepec Park.

BOTE PATEADO

Mexican children enjoy playing a version of hide-and-seek called bote pateado. At least three players are needed.

1. The players choose one person to be It. That person stands at the starting place. A can inside a drawn circle marks the starting place. Another player kicks the can as far from the circle as possible. The It player must walk to the can and walk it back to the circle. Running is not allowed. Meanwhile, the other players hide.

2. The It player starts looking for the others. When the It player finds someone hiding, the It player has to run back to the starting place. The remaining players can hide in a new spot. The found player stands in the circle.

3. The It player looks for another person.

4. The It player and the second found player race back to the can. If the found player reaches the can first, the person in the circle is free to hide again. If not, both players are stuck in the circle.

5. The game ends when everyone has been found and is stuck in the circle.

Mexico is a fascinating country. Visitors can go on adventures. The music and food offer a peek into many cultures. The traditions show the diversity that makes Mexico special.

GLOSSARY

ancestor (AN-sess-tur)
a relative that a person came from

annex (an-EKS)
to take control of a territory

BCE/CE
BCE means Before Common Era, or before year one. CE means Common Era, or the years starting with year one

conquistador (kon-KEYS-tuh-dor)
a 16th-century military leader from Spain

indigenous (in-DIJ-uh-nuhs)
the first people, plants, and animals to live in a country

irrigation (eer-uh-GAY-shun)
a method of using channels or pipes to carry water to crops

Mass (MAS)
a Catholic church service

patron saint (PAY-truhn SAYNT)
a person the Christian church has recognized as having lived a holy life and who is said to look after people or places

revolt (ri-VOHLT)
to rebel and try to overthrow a ruler

READ MORE

Loria, Laura. *La Malinche: Indigenous Translator for Hernán Cortés in Mexico*. New York: Britannica Educational Publishing, 2018.

Williams, Heather. *Soccer: A Guide for Players and Fans*. North Mankato, MN: Capstone, 2020.

Yasuda, Anita. *Ancient Civilizations: Aztecs, Maya, Incas!* White River Junction, VT: Nomad Press, 2019.

INTERNET SITES

Britannica Kids: Mexico
kids.britannica.com/students/article/Mexico/275813

National Geographic Kids: Mexico
kids.nationalgeographic.com/geography/countries/article/mexico

Wonderopolis: What Happened to the Maya?
wonderopolis.org/wonder/what-happened-to-the-maya

INDEX

ABOUT THE AUTHORS

Isela Xitlali Gómez R. is an East LA/Inland Empire transplant based in Minneapolis, Minnesota. She is a 2015 winner of the Loft Literary Center's Mentor Series in Creative Nonfiction, a 2017 Beyond the Pure Fellow through Intermedia Arts, and a 2020 fellow of the Loft Literary Center's Mirrors and Windows program.

Anaïs Deal-Márquez is a multidisciplinary artist raised in Mexico and the upper Midwest. She just finished the manuscript of her first poetry collection, which looks at memory, displacement, home, healing, and migration. She has been published in *Poetry* magazine, *The BreakBeat Poets Volume 4: LatiNEXT,* and elsewhere.

OTHER BOOKS IN THIS SERIES

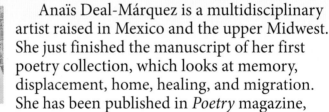

YOUR PASSPORT TO ARGENTINA
YOUR PASSPORT TO AUSTRALIA
YOUR PASSPORT TO CHINA
YOUR PASSPORT TO ECUADOR
YOUR PASSPORT TO EGYPT
YOUR PASSPORT TO EL SALVADOR
YOUR PASSPORT TO ENGLAND
YOUR PASSPORT TO ETHIOPIA
YOUR PASSPORT TO FRANCE
YOUR PASSPORT TO GUATEMALA

YOUR PASSPORT TO IRAN
YOUR PASSPORT TO ITALY
YOUR PASSPORT TO KENYA
YOUR PASSPORT TO PERU
YOUR PASSPORT TO RUSSIA
YOUR PASSPORT TO SOUTH KOREA
YOUR PASSPORT TO SPAIN
YOUR PASSPORT TO SRI LANKA
YOUR PASSPORT TO TURKEY